THE CROSS IS LIFTED

May you find some dew of rest in some line of this book after hard days of service.

Chaska

The Cross
is Lifted

by CHANDRAN DEVANESEN

DRAWINGS BY FRANK WESLEY

Friendship Press　•　*New York*

LIBRARY OF CONGRESS CATALOG CARD NO. 54-6193

First Printing May 1954
Second Printing October 1954

TEXT: LINOTYPE FAIRFIELD 11/13
COMPOSITION: THE COMPOSING ROOM, INC.
PRINTING: GENERAL OFFSET COMPANY
CLOTH BINDING: CHAS. H. BOHN & CO., INC.
PAPER BINDING: MERCURY BOOKBINDING SERVICE, INC.
MANUFACTURED IN NEW YORK

FORMAT AND BINDING DESIGN: LOUISE E. JEFFERSON

Printed in the United States of America

Contents

FOREWORD

"The gospel is a seed that is sown in the soil of a culture. The plant bears the marks both of the seed and the soil. There is one gospel; there are many Christianities. In Asian countries, Christianity is a potted plant which needs to be rooted in the cultural soil of the East." So said the Reverend Dr. D. T. Niles of Ceylon, speaking to a group of Asian student leaders. This collection of poems by my good friend, Chandran Devanesen, with illustrations by Frank Wesley, is an indication of a Christianity that is taking root in the cultural soil of India. Behind it lies the conviction that the salvation of India and her culture rests in Christ.

These poems and pictures are full of imageries and symbolisms that belong to the heart of India's cultural and religious tradition. The religious seeker in pilgrimage, the yellow robes, the singing of lyrics, the offering of flowers, the Lord's lotus feet, the temples and shrines—all these echo the deep religious past of India. To the American reader the meaning of these symbolisms cannot become clear at the first rapid glance. One must, therefore, ask for some effort at understanding.

There is, however, another side. While the artists stand within the cultural stream of India, they are expressing not a distant frozen past but a flowing stream; and this art represents the living present of the modern Indian renaissance. Indian youth today is marked, not by a world-negation of the proverbial East but by a world-affirmation that drinks deep in the beauty of nature and finds delight in earthly existence. This in a sense is a revolutionary break with the past. No one who enters into the spirit of these poems and paintings will miss the fact that our artists stand within this present with those who seek images and forms, both old and new, to express the new sense of reality of the world of nature, of the meaningfulness of human existence, and of joy in both. But both poet and artist are Christian in that they see in Christ the source and fulfilment of modern India's revolutionary experience of the love of life. These poems and pictures are filled with the imageries that express an enjoyment of nature and human friendship as well as a social humanism with its passionate concern for suffering humanity.

The question may be justly asked, where in all these is the Christ who judges culture? Have poet and artist reckoned with the gloomy realities of man's nature, the possible tragedy of his hopes? Notes that intimate a grappling with this deeper dimension of human culture and Christian faith are not absent in these poems. The poet is not unaware of the "meek and terrible Judge of all the earth" and His mercy from beyond it.

I believe that of all the poems in this collection, the "Lines to a Rickshaw Puller" is the best. Anyone in this country who wants to know the social and religious situation of India, the problem of proclaiming Christ to the peasant and worker, as well as the secret of the appeal of communism for them, must read and reread this piece. Without home, without property, eking out a meager existence by degrading toil that puts man on a par with the horse and the bullock is expressed in the picture of the rickshaw puller. His resentment against society has made him an unconscious communist before he has even heard of communism. This is the basic revolt of the people of India—the revolt against the denial of human dignity. The shadows of the rickshaw and the puller so suggestively painted by Frank Wesley are the writings on the wall. And the poet brings out both the complete lack of communication between the church and the Indian laborer and the impotence of the church to proclaim the gospel in the modern situation. And both the laborer and the Christian carry on a status quo in which both put on masks to cover resentment or fear; and humanity and brotherhood are denied by the dime paid and received.

Our wise men have not yet seen the star, . . .

> *Pass it on to the ends of the earth*
> *Christ is the answer—ours! yours!*

M. M. THOMAS

New York, New York
January 17, 1954

THE CROSS IS LIFTED

Two thousand years have slipped by
like freshets in the Ganges
since St. Thomas came to our land.
Here, though the cross is lifted
amidst the paddy fields and coconut palms
and white-clad Christians flock to the churches
when the bells call them to worship;
our wise men have not yet seen the star
and the manger of Bethlehem
is not yet the cradle of our land.
But Christian hope never dies
and the ends of the strands of destiny
are held safe in the hands of God.

*   *   *   *   *

Pass it on to the ends of the earth!
Christ is the answer—Ours! Yours!

Lord,
let me come
to Thee.

LITTLENESS

As a little bird
flies into the leafy vastness
of a tree,
as a little rivulet
flows into the swelling vastness of a sea,
as a little seed
sinks into the spreading vastness
of the earth,
Lord,
let me come
to Thee.

MORNING PRESENCE

O Thou
who hast given me eyes
to see the light
that fills my room,
give me the inward vision
to behold Thee in this place.

O Thou
who hast made me to feel
the morning wind upon my limbs,
help me to feel Thy Presence
as I bow in worship
of Thee.

INVOCATION

O Thou,
whom my soul adores,
draw near unto me
and bless me with Thy Presence.

As the moon is hidden
by the leaves of a tree,
so art Thou hidden from me
by my own desires.

Even when my soul
is as dark as night,
may the light of Thy beauty
shine through like the stars.

Fill Thou my heart
with the light of Thy Presence
until it glows like the dawn.

Fill Thou my eyes
with the light of Thy Presence
until I see naught else but Thee.

O Thou, who art
my prayer,
my praise,
my worship.

BARRENNESS

O Lord,
from the barren soil of my heart
may there yet spring a wondrous flower
of praise and worship
for Thee.
From the barren silence of my soul
may there yet spring a trilling bird
full of sweet songs
for Thee.

SEND YOUR ROOTS DEEP DOWN

O Tree of Calvary,
send your roots deep down
into my heart.
Gather together the soil of my heart,
the sands of my fickleness,
the stones of my stubbornness,
the mud of my desires.
Bind them all together,
O Tree of Calvary,
interlace them with Thy strong roots,
entwine them with the network
of Thy love.

STRANGE FLAMES

My heart is lit
by strange flames
and its withered grasses
crackle in their heat.
The winds of passion
blow through the dead branches
of its leafless trees
blazing an ocherous trail
for strange flames
that leap and dance
with fiendish glee
in my heart.

I burn, O Lord,
for strange flames
lick with devouring tongues
at all that grows
within my heart.
Save me, O Lord,
from these raging fires
that consume my inmost being.
Send down Thy heavenly rain
of tender mercy,
wet me through and through
with Thy torrential love
till every strange flame
is banished for ever
from my scorched heart.

THE BLUE LOTUS

Lord, I stoop to take the dust
from Thy nail-torn feet,
the bloody dust I see but dimly
through a mist of tears.
I stoop, in gratitude I stoop,
to touch Thy feet,
for I have entered into the fellowship
of Thy sufferings.

I wanted my heart to be a lake,
a laughing lake studded with lotuses,
red lotuses of joy
and white lotuses of purity.
Ah, my heart is a lake indeed—
a lake of salt tears!
A dark lake where grows a lonely lotus,
the blue lotus of pain.

I stoop and lay my precious lotus,
the lotus culled from my sad heart at Thy feet.
Thy red blood trickles over its blue petals,
and my suffering becomes a part
of Thine own immemorial pain.
Lord, I do not understand
the mystery of life's immortal pain.
But I thank Thee for this lotus,
this blue lotus that has laid me also in the dust
before Thy lotus feet.

I found Faith....
Hope....
Love....

DISCOVERY

When a little child
laid its head upon my shoulder
I found Faith . . . .

When a blind man smiled
despite his sightless eyes
I found Hope . . . .

When a wooden cross
bore a broken body upon it
I found Love . . . .

ALTAR FLOWERS

In chapel tonight
I suddenly became aware
of the flowers
on the altar
as I had never been aware
of them
before.
There is nothing in my life
comparable to the beauty
of these humble blooms
of red hibiscus.
What am I in the presence
of these exquisite tokens
of Thy divine artistry?
The shabbiness of my life
can offer Thee no worship
like unto the silent praise
of these flowers
on the altar.

DARSHAN

Lord,
so eager was I for Thy *darshan*
that I donned the yellow robes of a *sannyasi*.
I walked the dusty, weary miles
of the road from Dravida to the Himalayas
in my bare feet.

I endured the heat of noonday,
the lash of monsoon tempests,
the perils of tortuous jungle paths.
Lonely forest shrines echoed to my *kirtans*
when I offered *puja* with garlands of wild flowers.
But nowhere did I find Thee . . . .

And then suddenly I met Thee,
met Thee walking the roads
of my own heart.

BHARATA NATYAM

Lord,
we thank Thee
for the sublime art
of *Bharata natyam*.
We thank Thee for the suppleness
of body and limb
and the gracefulness of fingers
shaped in a *mudra*.
As we dwell upon the quick movements
of the dancers
and the color of the costumes;
as we listen to the music
and the jingle of the anklets of bells,
may we realize Thee
in the dance.

For Thou art He that sits among us
on the stage of Life
beating the *tabla* to which we keep time.
Thine is the orchestra
which sets the pattern of the moods
we express in quick or slow rhythm.
And Thou art in the climax
towards which the whole dance moves.

IMMANUEL

God of God . . . .
    Only the sound of an infant
    crying in the night,
    a familiar, homely, human sound
    like the sound of hooves on flagstones,
    like the rattle of chains tethering cattle,
    like the crunch of straw in the mouths of oxen,
    like the rustle of hay tossed into a manger.

Light of light . . . .
    Only the light of a star
    falling on an infant in a crib
    like the light in a shepherd's lantern,
    like the light in the eyes of a mother,
    like the light in the learning of wise men,
    like the light that lightens each dawn.

Very God of very God . . . .
    Only a pillow of straw
    and an infant in rags and tatters
    like the weather-worn blankets of shepherds,
    like dusty, travel-stained garments of travelers,
    like old clothes thrown to a beggar,
    like cloths stuffed in a stable window
    to keep the draught out and cattle warm.

God is with us,
terribly, simply with us.
And the shadows of men
with arms outstretched to take Him
fall across the manger
in the form of a cross.

THE INFINITE CHRIST

Lord,
I am a painter
and Thou
art my subject.

My mind is my spreading canvas.
My imagination is my strong brush.
I mix my colors lavishly,
rainbow colors stolen from flower's heart
and seashell's shiny texture.
I catch with delight
the red of dust
that rises about the hooves of cattle
and gold filtered from sunlight
that soaks through the clouds.
I daub and splash,
Ah so rapturously!
I fashion line and form,
Ah so cunningly!
I differentiate tint from tint,
Ah so delicately!
I bring out all the nuance of light and shade,
Ah so deftly!

Lord,
I am a painter
and Thou
art my subject.

But my portrait will never be complete
for Thou art infinite
like the eternal color-pageant
of Nature.

Lord,
I am a musician
and Thou
art my music.

My thoughts have fingers
that tug at the taut fibers
of my being, releasing
sound upon sound.
The breath of my mind
rushes through the flute
of my body
in cadence upon cadence.

Lord,
I am a musician
and Thou
art my music.
But my music will never be complete
till I have imprisoned every sound
in the eternal, fugitive tunes
of Nature.

CHRIST AND MAYA

Lord Christ,
Thou hast broken the lure of my *maya*.
Thou hast clothed this earthly illusion
with the garment of Thine own splendid Self
making this Unreal into Thy Real.
Thou hast imprisoned me in the net
of Thy beauty.
Thou hast dazzled my eyes
with the spell of Thy loveliness.
When I look at the *shimul* tree
I see Thy heart in every red blossom.
Thine eyes are in the stars
that dance with the lotuses upon the moon-lit pools.
Thy voice is in the whisper among the *kusum* leaves.
I hear Thee in the drowsy tune
played by a drowsy boy
in the mango *tope* where the cows are straying.
I see Thee in the eyes of every beggar.
I see Thee in the leprous skin of the leper.
I see Thee passing through every village street.
I see Thee striding along our roads
with the red dust rising about Thy heels.
Thou art terrible
when Thy voice is in the roaring of monsoon gales,
when Thy righteous anger flashes in the lightning.
Thou art gentle
when Thou art in the hand
that helps to take a load from off a tired coolie's head,
When Thou art in the kiss

a young mother gives to her first-born.
Ah Lord Christ,
Thy Form ever dances before my eyes.
Thou hast veiled my eyes
with the veils of Thine eternal delight.
Thou hast thrown dust in my eyes,
the precious dust of Thine own secret joy.

THY YOKE

O Lord, Thy yoke is easy
and Thy burden light,
but my neck is obstinate
and my back unbending.
My eyes wander from the paths
in which Thou wouldst direct me
to green grasses of distraction
and tempting leaves of desire.
When Thou dost want me to run
I stumble and fall.
When Thou dost want me to walk
I lie down to chew the cud
of idleness.
O Lord, forgive my stubbornness
and my foolish ways.

Be patient with me
Till I have learned Thy discipline
in the gentle pull of Thy rope
which is my true comfort and freedom.

I feel the pain. . . .

OF HUMAN BONDAGE

The hounds are baying.
I hear their baying across the centuries
borne on the howling winds of hate
that have filled the world.
Their deep-throated cry chills my blood
and their bared fangs, their foam-flecked jowls
fill my eyes with terror.
I hear the hoarse cries,
the snarls, the angry shouts,
the cruel din of man's history.
I see the upraised knout,
I hear it come whistling down
on writhing, bare backs
to the accompaniment of mad, sadistic laughter.
I feel the pain of leathern thongs
that cut into the flesh
of struggling hands.
I see the hideous, brute faces
lit by the leaping flames.
I hear the sobs, the wails, the screams,
all the movements in the grim concerto
of agonized humanity.
I smell the acrid smell
of burning human flesh.
And the tears are salt, and the blood is red,
like the blood that dripped
from Thy hands and feet,
from Thy speared side
onto the green grass of Golgotha.

20

FRAGMENT FROM GOLGOTHA

My mind is for ever splintered
on the anvil of Time
and my spirit wanders restlessly
through the caverns of Eternity.
You ask me why?
I was an ordinary legionary in Jerusalem
nigh two thousand years ago.
One chill, windy morning
we nailed a Man to a cross.
(It was a routine job.)
He died rather soon.
I remember throwing down the dice
(we were gambling for His clothes),
and, picking up my spear, a trusty weapon
that had seen me through many a skirmish
in Gaul and Libya,
I thrust it into His side
to make certain before telling the centurion.
I saw water and blood trickle down the haft
gripped in my hands.
I saw more—though, by the bird of Jupiter,
I wish I hadn't.
Looking into His deathless eyes
I saw His heart was broken
for me.

THOUGHTS FROM THE SKY

Evening came wandering slowly
into our shadow-haunted mango grove
like some old *rishi* come to worship.
Silence dripped from the quietened leaves
and every blade of grass was still.
Overhead crowds of attendant clouds
were trimming the lamps of heaven.
The sky drew closer to the earth
to hush it to sleep.
Looking at the vast expanse above
I remembered how the ancients
on the plains of Aryavarta
had called it *Om*.

Om! Our lips scarce form the word
ere it speeds forth, vibrant as an arrow,
and goes winging past the stars
to the uttermost boundaries of the universe.

22

Om! one mystic syllable
that sends the mind rippling across pools of space,
along endlessly reverberant tracks of sound
that lead to the mouth of God.

Om! God in a sound
that is murmurous with the music
of eternity . . . .

Suddenly the dewy air distilled a sound
as of a thousand bees in humming flight.
An aeroplane sped past on outstretched wings
that were strangely motionless:
another word came crashing ruthlessly
into the peace of my mind.

Bomb! all the difference between heaven and hell!
Man spreads machine wings
that mount him to the skies;
the upward look of awe
turns into the downward look of contempt.
Man's screech of achievement
comes whistling down, ear-deafening,
in the shape of a bomb!

THE MIGHTY ATOM

Now has man become the mighty atom,
and his laughter is terrible and pitiless.
He has filched the power in the stars
for his thunderbolts of death.
He stalks the earth breathing fire from his mouth
and the smell of roasted human flesh
is sweet to his nostrils.
The earth hangs from his parachute of power
as if it is doomed to destruction.
Now has man become the mighty atom
and his suicidal fury assails the universe.

But through the pall of radio-active smoke
that seethes from earth to heaven
I see Thy form upon the cross,
Thou meek and terrible judge of all the earth.
I see Thy wounds in the burning blood,
I feel Thy pain in the broken bodies of men.
in the midst of the roaring devastation,
I hear Thy voice
"Forgive thine enemies, do good to them
that hate you."

CRUCIFIXION

Jesus looked down from the cross,
with a heart breaking for all mankind,
two thousand years ago.
Dark tides of hatred whirled about Him.
Stark, elemental forces shook the world.
Thick darkness veiled the trembling earth.
Jesus cried in agony, "Father forgive them
for they know not what they do."
Jesus looked down from the cross,
with a heart breaking for all mankind,
in A.D. 1943.
Huge fleets of bombers blotted out the stars.
Children ran to air raid shelters
in the lurid glow of incendiaries.
The earth shook under the weight of tanks.
The sea refused to give up its dead.
Jesus cried in agony, "Father forgive them
for they know not what they do."

And so I pass
from flower and grass
to the very essence
of His holy Presence....

HEDGES

When I see a single flower
blooming in lonely splendor
in the midst of a thorny hedge
I stop and gaze at it
in silent admiration.
When I glimpse a truth of God,
a single bloom of wisdom
in a hedgerow of life's perplexities,
I stop and bow my head in silent adoration.
And so I pass
from flower and grass
to the very essence
of His holy Presence.
The hedgerows of earth
are the battlements of heaven.

DAWN

O Lord of the dawn,
may my heart fill with Thy praise
when Thy light fills the skies.
O Thou, who art in the morning light,
may the light of each new dawn
reveal Thee to me more clearly.
O Thou, who art in the night-cooled breeze,
may I hear Thy morning laughter in the trees.
O Thou, who art in the rising sun
hear my morning salutation,
listen to the Matins of my heart.

THE RIVER

O river,
rushing down the hills,
would that your falling, flashing spirit
lent speed to my motionless self,
for I have lost myself
in stagnant sloughs of deadness.
I am listening to you, laughing river,
as you hasten along.
The voices of your many waters
are tinkling merrily
as they roll the pebbles,
they are singing gleefully
as they leap from boulder to boulder,
they are humming softly
as they cascade from pool to pool.
Oh, the green banks of my selfish desires
that shut me in my prison
of mud and weeds, weeds and mud!
I lie awake at night
and hear you crooning cradle songs
to the restless stars
that rock on your bosom.

O river, river,
how quickly you race through the shallows,
how boldly you flow through the deeps,
how loudly you chant on your pilgrimage
as you twist and turn, leap and churn
your way to the sea.

THE DIVINE GARDENER

When the evening sun
was twisting the shadows
into long, slow gestures of farewell
I stood looking at the flowers
in my small garden.
And I beheld the Lord
smiling at my side.
He laughed and said,
"I sow My spirit-seed
in the hearts of men
and rejoice when they blossom forth
in soul-flowers."

SEASIDE MEDITATION

Forgive me, O Lord,
for the ships of my soul
spread glad sails to the wind
only to be wrecked on rocks
that lie hid in depths of selfishness.
Forgive me, O Lord,
for the voyages of my mind
are like those of frail *catamarans*
that cling to familiar coasts
and dare not venture out
where the landmarks of green palms
are lost to sight.

THE STAR TURNS RED

A star once flashed into our skies
to herald a new-born king,
a strange king who came in lowly guise,
a frail child all wrapped in swaddling clothes
who was to reign supreme
in the wide domain of human hearts.
It was a star whose light was peopled
with a radiancy of angelic choirs,
singing peace and goodwill
to all who dwell upon this our earth.

And He who broods upon the universe
has waited long to see our planet
rise, star-like, in His skies
all flushed with victory,
the victory of the Child who came as Love.
But while He waits
no starriness our earth o'ertakes.
It only sickens and turns red,
red with human blood and suffering.
Oh, when will rise our earth
clear and pure as a star,
joyful as a second Christmas night
to make the Father laugh with child delight?

DAWN IN TAMBARAM

The morning breeze is a playful dog
rushing through my garden
with a lolling tongue of pink cloud.
He springs upon the flame of the forest
filling her with mirth.
She waves her bare arms
and raises her hands to the skies
laden with her offering of red flowers.
A brown rabbit hops out of the tall grasses,
his long ears quivering,
his eyes full of meditation.
A mongoose lopes along
stopping every now and then
to throw a backward look
at the way he came,
a symbol of eternal vigilance.
When the first rays of the sun
streak across the horizon
the birds cease their chatter
and form a sweet-throated choir
trilling matutinal songs that mount upwards,
a swift-winged crescendo of praise.
And I, gazing at the sea of green shrubbery
also give Thee thanks, O Christ,
for the life that springs
in tree and beast and bird,
that awakens at Thy touch
and grows in the light of Thy love.

CHILD'S SONG

When Jesus walked in Galilee
little birds sang to Him,
little birds flew to Him
and hopped about His feet.
When Jesus walked in Galilee
autumn leaves danced for Him,
autumn leaves floated to Him
and fluttered to His feet.
When Jesus walked by Galilee
little waves crept to Him,
little waves ran to Him
and kissed His tired feet.

SEASONS

I thank Thee for Pain,
the sister of Joy.
I thank Thee for Sorrow,
the twin of Happiness.

Pain, Joy, Sorrow, Happiness.
Four angels at work on the Well of Love.

Pain and Sorrow dig it deep with aches.
Joy and Happiness fill it up with tears
that come with smiles.

For the seasons of emotion in my heart,
I thank Thee, O Lord.

TREES

Trees
in the heat of noonday
spread their carpet of shade for Him
and fanned Him with their cool breezes.

Trees
in the cool of night
covered Him with mantles of checkered moonlight
and sheltered Him from the dew.

Trees
in the pelting rain
hung their great branches over Him
to keep Him out of the wet.
And when He bled on Calvary
a tree shared His agony.

THE LORD'S COMPASSION

Lord,
the stars float from Thy hands
like silver bubbles.
The clouds wrap themselves round Thy fingers.
Rivers flow across Thy palms
which are covered with miles of forest and green fields
and lakes that have formed in their hollows.
Suns flash from Thy forehead.
Universes dance about Thy feet . . . .

And yet, O Lord,
Thou didst tread the dusty road
that led to Golgotha.
Thou didst hang upon a cruel cross
for love of mere men.

COONOOR

O hills of my delight,
the noisy tumults of my life
hush into silence
before your quiet majesty.
The white clouds drift past your summits
into my parched heart
bringing the cool rain
of penitential tears,
tears that clear my eyes
till I can see in every hill a Calvary.

SILENCE

My silence is a sky
which Thou dost adorn
with beauteous stars.
My silence is a grove
which Thou dost fill
with songbirds.
My silence is a rosary
that clicks to the rhythm
of Eternity.
My silence is a pearl,
a pearl forming secretly
which Thou wilt give to me.

—

NIGHT

Lord, I thank Thee for night,
the time of cool and quiet,
the time of sweet enchantment
when a deep mystery pervades everything.
The time when soul speaks to soul in common desire
to partake of the hush of the ineffable.
The time when the moon and the stars
speak to man of his high calling and destiny.
The time of repose and calm
when the fever of the mind subsides
and uncertainty gives place
to the sense of eternal purpose.
O Lord, I thank Thee for night.

CEYLON (The Jeweled Isle)

The yellow sand is a strand of gold
laved by a sapphire sea.
The coconut palms lean their bronze trunks
against the balustrade of wind
tossing their tresses of emerald and jade.
The sky is a moonstone of misty blue
flecked with delicate veins of white cloud.
The amber boats with their russet sails
plunge like restless horses in the ivory foam.
A red glow suffuses earth and sky
as the dying sun sheds his ruby blood
into the goblet of the sea.
The purple twilight veils the naked limbs
of day against the hungry eyes of darkness
night falls over Eden.

IMMORTALITY

O bee,
the fierce tremor
of your passionate wings
sings a love song to the flowers
that is born of a thousand years.

O bee,
when I am no more,
when a thousand years hence
this earthly part of me
lives in the scent of flowers,
methinks I will hear you again
charming my listening petals
with the music of your wings,
and capture with delight
the tune you hum in the air today.

SPIRITUS SANCTUS

O Spirit of God, mighty river,
flow over me, in me, through me.
O Spirit of God, cleanse me,
purify the channels of my life.
O Spirit of God, bear me along
with Thy flood of life-giving service.
O Spirit of God, mighty river,
bear me down to the ocean,
the ocean of Thy Love.

O Spirit of God, mighty fire,
glow in me, burn in me
until Thy radiance fills my soul.
O Spirit of God, mighty fire,
may Thy light illumine my mind.
O Spirit of God, mighty fire,
may Thy heat consume my will
until I burn for Thee.
May the flames of Thy Love
ever blaze upon the altar
of my heart.

. . . the love I taste from Thee
is the love that is in my love
for others, and the love that others
have for me.

THE POSTMAN'S KNOCK

Sometimes the book I'm reading
   falls from my hands
   and treasure-laden argosies of thought
   bear me across seas of purpling splendor.

Sometimes eternity spreads before me
   like a vast field of flowers
   where the years of my life
   seem like small boys chasing butterflies
   through meadow gateways of heaven.

Sometimes I gaze upon Thee
   in all Thy manifold beauty
   until I become oblivious of all else
   and time becomes a distant sense
   like the unconscious throbbing of a pulse.

Then comes the postman's knock.
I greet him with a smile
   for his knock reminds me
   of the time of day,
   of births, deaths, and marriages,
   of the calendar of local events,
   of bitterness and sweetness,
   of joy and sorrow—
   all the alternating lights and shades
   of daily human history.

And then I know, O Lord
   that the love I taste from Thee
   is the love that is in my love
   for others, and the love that others
   have for me.

Even as eternity is measured
   by Thy hands on a clock
   so is Thy love measured to us
   in the measure with which we love,
   until love speaks to perfect Love
   without fear.

MOTHER INDIA

O India, Mother,
why the tears upon your cheek?
Why this sorrow in your heart?
Is it your long travail,
your immemorial agony?
Is it the pain of hope deferred,
the anguish of despair?
Lift, Mother, lift up your face.
Let your eyes catch the light,
the light that streams from a star,
the Star of Bethlehem.
Surely the quickening life in you
will come to fruition in a Saviour
who will bring you your heart's joy
as He did to the lowly Mary,
purest of Asia's daughters.
Ah, Mother,
Bala Yesu would be born in you.
He would play at your knee.
He would walk our dusty roads
and lie under our palms.
O India, Mother,
cradle Him in your heart!
He will fill your longing soul with great gladness.

ADVENT

Art Thou a stranger to my country, Lord?
My land of black rocks and thick jungles
where the wild boar sharpens his tusks,
where the monkeys chatter in the trees,
and the peacock's shrill note
echoes through the mist-clad hills;
my land of brown, caked river mud
where the elephant and the leopard come to drink,
and the shambling bear with his dreamy eyes
sees the porcupine shedding his quills;
my land with its friezes of palmyra palms
etched sharply against the blue mountains;
my land of low-lying plains
with its miles of murmuring paddy fields
that stretch in undulating waves of green
to the distant horizon;
my land of sapphire skies and flaming sunsets,
my land of leaden gray skies piled high
with banks of monsoon clouds;
my land of stinging rain, of burning heat,
of dark nights, of enchanted moons
that dance behind the coconut fronds;
my land of tanks and pools
where the lazy buffalo wallows
and the red lotuses lie asleep?
Nay, Thou art no stranger, Lord,
for the wind whispers of Thee
and the waters chant Thy Name.
The whole land is hushed in trembling expectancy,
awaiting Thy touch of creative Love.

45

LINES TO A RICKSHAW PULLER

I pass you every morning
on my way to the station.
The light is raw and the wind is keen.
All around you the city is stretching its limbs
and wiping the sleep from its eyes.
The raucous voice of the crow is everywhere.
But you hear nothing, you see nothing.
You lie curled up in your rickshaw
with sprawling limbs and inert body
like some tired animal.
Some mother must have cradled you
pressing you against the soft comfort
of her warm breasts.
But now you shape your body
to fit the wooden embrace
of the hard sides of your rickshaw
for its walls are your home, your rented home.
Your intimacy with it is very great.
Your worldly possessions are in the box
under the seat with its torn fibre cushion
keeping company with your oil lamps,
the battered old *topee*

you wear on rainy days,
and a few *beedis*.
The shafts are worn smooth
by the contact of your forearms.
The rickshaw and you—
you belong together.
I have passed you by at other times—
when you were not asleep
and something of your life
has trailed after me.
I remember the laughter of your fellows
as you twitted the grain seller
who sits by the rickshaw stand
until the old hag exposed her gums
in a toothless grin. . . .
I have watched you fight with your creditors
with the ferocity of a trapped beast
over pitiful sums, the price of a packet of fags.
I have heard you whine for a fare
when the day's earnings were poor.
I have seen you resentful and bitter
when you spat on the ground
and talked unconscious communism.
I pass you by like a hundred others
who also pass you by—
and the road may be the road
from Jerusalem to Jericho for all we know.
I would like to put my hand on your shoulder
and say to you, "Comrade,
there is One who died for us
and dying made us blood brothers."

But I am filled with the cowardice of the well-dressed—
for clothes are by no means flimsy
when it comes to erecting barriers
between man and man.
I am afraid you will wake with a start
and betray resentment in your eyes
as you see in me what I really am—
your well-dressed enemy.
And then you will acknowledge defeat
and put on your mask of patient stupidity.
You will jump up and dust the seat
and grin and point to it with a flourish of your hand.
You will want us to sell our brotherhood
for eight *annas*.

Day after day I pass you by,
you the man by the roadside
and I the priest and the Levite rolled in one,
passing you by.

THE SONG OF THE LOVERS

O Love divine, beauteous Spirit,
in trembling ecstasy
we sing our song
of praise to Thee.

O Thou, who made us,
formed us from the same substance
of the earth and the stars,
gave us bodies filled with life,
with the sap in trees,
with the power to sprout and blossom,
to put forth buds of tenderness
and flowers of passion,
we thank Thee for giving us
to each other.
O timeless mystery of Love,
that formed us of primeval mud,
that drew us from fresh earth,

49

that shaped our limbs through centuries,
that made us man and woman
with a hunger for each other
till we stood side by side
like two trees with roots intertwined,
like two trees with interlacing branches,
we thank Thee for this bliss
of living, growing sweet communion.
O Spirit of enchantment and delight,
Thou who has veiled us
with shining aureoles of secret joy,
Thou who has bound us
with the spell of wonder,
Thou who hast opened for us
the casements of mystic rapture
flooding us with light and love,
we thank Thee for this unfolding vision
of each other.

O Creator of the life within us,
for the pain of parting,
for the sacrament of meeting,
for the warmth of homely intimacy
and the fire of love's ritual,
we give Thee ardent thanks
and all our gratitude.

> O Love divine, beauteous Spirit,
> in trembling ecstasy
> we sing our song
> of praise to Thee.

CHRIST OF THE INDIAN ROAD

Have you not heard about Him,
O my brothers?
Do you not know about Him,
O my sisters?

He was a carpenter.
The wood yielded to His hands.
His yokes were easy upon the ox's neck,
and sweat was upon His brow.
He called Himself the Son of Man.
He did not despise the *devadasi*.
He cared for the beggar and the dog
That licked the beggar's sores.
He brought sight to the blind
and healed the leper.
He cured the diseased in mind
and gave them new life .   .   .   .

He gives a dream that will not
let a young man sleep.

51

He gives an adventure that will not
let a young man rest .   .   .   .

He can give you life that is as bread
to your hungry bellies.
Listen to Him, O *babu*, toiling in your office.
He can give you life that is as hours
spent away from your desk .   .   .   .

Listen to Him, O men and women of India,
you and your children.
The hands that are His
will speed the plow through our fields of poverty.
The minds that are His
will create the plan which hums
in the roar of the city,
which throbs in the rhythm of the *tabla*
beaten in the village.
The hearts that are His
will clear the way and build the
road that is gentle even to crippled feet.
Let Him lead us in the march of Humanity,
to the wonder that awaits,
to the eye-unseen, the ear-unheard Future
that leads over star-track and Beyond!

ONE OF THE TWELVE

He was pale and handsome
with a shock of red hair
that glowed on his head
like a danger signal.
His fingers were long and tapering
but they twitched nervously.
He kept wiping his hands on his robe
as if there was a stain on them
that refused to come off.

Now what was there one noticed about his face?
It wasn't effeminate; it wasn't cruel;
no, it wasn't even sensual.
     Then what was it?
It was a weak face.
Yes, that's what it was—
a weakness in the line of his mouth,
in the abutment of his chin.

He looked so young and almost helpless
that you couldn't help pitying him.
He had a hollow, despairing sort of laugh.
He bit his nails, looked furtively at his palms,
and told me he had been a traitor.

It was funny, he said,
but the Man he had betrayed
had often pitied him.

Why did he betray Him?
Oh, for quite ordinary motives,
motives that are likely to suggest themselves
to any ordinary young man.
There was a woman involved.

There usually is—
when one is young and passionate.
That was the trouble with him.
He was always in a passion
about everything he did.
That's the trouble, he said, with all young men.
They are so passionate about everything.
And passion doesn't last—like love.

He may not have been conscious of it,
but he joined the Master
because he wanted this woman.

So many of us, he said rather defensively,
so many of us, mix up personal issues
with larger causes.

He was politically conscious, progressive;
he wanted to see his country free.
He hated the foreign oppressors.
And hating is as easy as loving
when you are young.
His master was to head the rebellion
that would break the foreign yoke forever.

He would be at the Master's side to see that He did.
His Master would be King,
but he would be King-maker.

That was his youthful dream.
That was his picture of the future
framed by the dark tresses
of the woman he loved.
That was why he was one
of the twelve.

He was always thinking of her
as he walked along with the twelve.
He would give her costly silks and perfumes.
He would give her chests of sandalwood
filled with precious stones,
and black Nubian slaves to wait upon her
as she stretched her sleek beauty
on a gem-studded couch . . . .
All this would he do when the Master was King.

There would be no more of this despicable
stealing from the common purse
to give her cheap little trinkets.

55

But day followed day, month followed month,
and nothing happened.
In vain did he rave
that it was wrong political strategy,
this knocking about in the countryside,
this dallying with hungry mobs
that clustered round them like flies,
when the seat of sovereign power was in Jerusalem.

And she was growing impatient
of his splendid dream.
She wanted him to buy a little field,
to build a little house,
to settle down.
Women do not like wanderers.
They like their men by the fireside.

And so he ate his heart out
until nothing was left but a black emptiness.
And in that void something moved,
something as black as the pit of hell,
as fascinatingly ugly as a snake.
It was the first thought of treachery.

Treachery, did he say?
But it didn't look like treachery then.
It was a superb bit of logic,
a perfect piece of rationalization.
His master said He was the Son of God.
Then how could earthly power harm Him?
He was not hindering but helping Him,

pushing Him into a dangerous situation
where He would have to assert Himself
and proclaim His kingly power.

It was such a neat and tidy little scheme.
His Master would get His kingdom,
and he would get his woman
her plot of land.

When he saw Him by the light of torches
among the olive trees on Gethsemane
and kissed Him, he did not think
it was the seal of death.

He thought it was a kiss of acclamation,
a heralding of kingly triumph.
He bought the little field for her.
It cost him all the thirty shekels of silver
which the High Priest had thrust
into his trembling hand.

But everything went wrong.
The clever little scheme broke down
pitilessly exposing the selfishness
hidden under the thick folds of rationalization.
Yes, it was plain, ordinary selfishness,
nothing monstrous, nothing villainous;
the ordinary selfishness of a young man
wrapped up in his love affair,
his worldly ambitions,
his pet political theories.

And yet it was the great betrayal of Love
by the selfish passions of youth.

　　He went to tell her what he'd done.
　　But she told him what he'd done,
　　with a horror in her eyes
　　that reflected three crosses on Golgotha.

It was then he really died
though later his body swung from a tree
in the pleasant little field meant for love,
the field of Aceldama, the field of blood.
And then it was that I noticed
the halter round his neck.

It was strange, he said,
the way he felt it was always there
when he had put it on.
He had woven it with his life,
his rope of destiny.
Before he turned to go
he said with a wan, ghostly smile
that his name was
　　　　Judas Iscariot.

THY KINGDOM COME

Asato ma sad gamaya—
> Out of Untruth lead us into Truth.

Lord, hear the cry of the civilized. Lead us from the untruth
in the mouth of the gun, the barking, sputtering gun, the
gun that silences the still, small voice of justice; the gun
which in the hands of the oppressed turns into the tyrant's
bayonet in the belly of the people.

Lead us from the untruth in the burr and whirr, the clack
and clatter of the Machine when it is made to grind the
people; from the smoke and soot, the cotton and dust which
coughs the blood from the lungs of the worker.

Lead us from the untruth of false ideals which drag history in the mud, and set our feet upon the road of Truth.

Tamaso ma jyotir gamaya—
> Out of Darkness lead us into Light.

Lord, lead us out of the darkness of the *kisan's* house of mud, the sweeper's home of kerosene tins, and the *chawls* and *bustees* of the factory worker, into the light of airy rooms and spacious parks and the sound of children playing in open spaces.

Lead us out of the darkness of the darkened mind which grades man by *namam* and *varnam* into high caste and low caste, the darkness of the hand outstretched to Thee which will not touch the skin of the *chuklis* and *pariahs,* the darkness of men who seek refuge in Thy shadow but refuse Thee in the shadow of Thy poor and lowly.

Lead us out of the darkness that plunges the girl into the darkness of an old man's desire, the darkness of the girl-pawn in the dowry shop; the darkness of the child robbed of her youth, of her years of blossoming into womanhood.

Lead us from the darkness of bondage into the light of freedom in the world of nations.

Lead us from the darkness of our today into the light of Thy tomorrow.

Mrityor ma mritam gamaya—
> Out of Death lead us into Eternity.

Lord, out of the death of evil thinking and evil doing lead
us into the eternity of the Good Life.

Out of the death of our own bodies lead us into the eternity
of the life of the race which springs from our flesh.

Lead us out of the death of the seen into the eternity of the
Unseen. When death approaches may we cry, *Santi! Santi!
Santi!* peace, deep peace, and so pass into the eternity of
the deathless Mind which is in the Form of all things.

Give them wide horizons . . . .

A PRAYER FOR THE YOUTH OF INDIA

Lord,
hear us, we pray Thee
for the young men and women of India.
Give them strong and healthy bodies
with which to fight the demons of disease
that ravage our land.
Give our young men broad shoulders and
full chests
and give both grace and strength to our
young women.
Give them clean vigorous minds
that are free from the menace of superstition
and the canker of prejudice.
Endow them with the power of reason
and sharpen their intellect,
but fill them with humility.

Give them the courage to face a challenge squarely,
to carry on when even hope seems dead,
and a high sense of adventure.
Give them the anodyne of humor
to take the sting out of adversity.
May they abhor a life that is without a purpose
and an outlook that does not comprehend service.
Give them a sense of vocation
and teach them the dignity of labor.
May they know the high aspirations
of a life centered in Thee
and the joy of work that is done in Thy name.
Grant that they may know the true meaning
of love and all its divine ecstasy,
and give them the courage to set for themselves
a new ideal of marriage
that will free our land
from the curse of dowries and child widows.
Sanctify their loves and make a true sacrament
of their marriages
so that they may be to each other true lovers and
friends and comrades of the road.
Teach them the art of building a home
with floors of cleanliness and walls of simplicity,
with windows that are open
for the sunshine of children,
the fresh air of friendship,
and hospitality that blooms like the *tulsi*.
Give to them an abundant love for country,
a patriotism that is free from sentimentality.
Hold Thou ever before them the ideal of service,

give them a willingness for cheerful sacrifice.
Give them a strong determination to rid us
of our manifold evils,
but temper their hatred for wrong with goodwill.
Make them bridgebuilders between the communi-
ties and peacemakers for Thee.
Help them to avoid the pitfall of slogans and catchwords.
Give them a sense of proportion, the gift of patience
to think out principles and standards and values
that will make for true and lasting freedom.
Teach them the good that is universal
and that which is everywhere equally true.
Make them fighters for world peace and brotherhood.
Give them the hope of a new world
and systems that are free from sin.
Give them wide horizons
that they may see beyond our country a planet
and beyond the planet the stars
and over and around them
and in and about them
the Kingdom of which Thou art Lord.

GLOSSARY

annas: coins worth about 1⅓ cents in American currency.

Aryavarta: an ancient name for India, the land of the Aryans.

Asato ma sad gamaya: "From the unreal lead me to the real."

babu: gentleman.

Bala Yesu: Child Jesus.

beedis: cheap Indian cigars.

Bharata Natyam: an Indian classical dance.

bustee: laborers' tenements, slums.

catamarans: native coasting vessels.

chawls: factory workers' tenements, slums.

chuklis: low-caste leather workers.

Coonoor: located in Nilgiri Hills in South India.

darshan: vision.

devadasi: harlot; literally a girl dedicated to the god of the temple.

Dravidia: South India, the home of Dravidians.

kirtans: lyrics.

kisan: peasant.

kusum: a tree in India.

maya: illusion; unreality.

Mrityor ma mritam gamaya: "From death lead me to immortality."

mudra: sign used in an Indian dance.

namam: name; an Indian name usually also indicates caste.

OM: a mystic syllable signifying divine reality.

pariahs: outcastes, untouchables.

puja: worship, offering.

rishi: ascetic, hermit.

sannyasi: religious mendicant.

santi: peace.

shimul: a tree in India.

tabla: a kind of drum.

Tamaso ma jyotir gamaya: "From darkness lead me to light."

Tambaram: the suburb of the city of Madras in South India.

tope: grove.

topee: hat.

tulsi: a plant of religious significance.

varnam: color, originally the basis of caste.

Chandran Devanesen was born in Palamcottah, South India, on November 1, 1917. He went to high school in Madras, attended Kingswood College, Kandy, Ceylon, and took his Master's Degree from Selwyn College, Cambridge, England. After graduation Mr. Devanesen was Youth Secretary of the National Christian Council of India, Burma, and Ceylon for two years, and he has been Professor of History at the Madras Christian College, Tambaram, for the last seven years. He was Chairman of the Student Christian Movement of India, Pakistan, and Ceylon for six years. He is married to a Singhalese woman from Ceylon and has three sons.

Mr. Devanesen is the author of *Prayers for Young Men, The Task of The Christian in the Asian University, The Infinite Christ* (a collection of poems), and *Communism and Christianity* (prepared in collaboration with Dr. J. F. Butler). All of these books were published by the Christian Literature Society, Madras, India.

THE ARTIST

Frank Wesley, whose drawings illustrate this book of poems, is most deeply interested in expressing Christian truth through Indian symbols. Coming from a family of mixed Hindu and Muslim descent, members of which have been Christians for three generations, his life is dedicated to Christian witness through his paintings. His pictures have been distributed throughout India under the auspices of the Christian Home Movement. Mr. Wesley is now studying Japanese traditional art, color-woodcut, and lacquer in Japan, developing new skills to use in the service of the church.